This page is intentionally left blank.

Interview: Oso Chanel, Lolita Chanel, Nova Stella, Onya Nerves
Introduction, Transcription, Editing: Brooke Shaffner
Cover Design, Layout: Niteesh Elias
Published by: Freedom Tunnel Press

ISBN-13: 979-8-9903495-0-6

Freedom Tunnel Press
Charlotte, NC, 28205
Printed and bound in Durham, North Carolina, USA

It's Soulful and It's Survival

A Conversation with Four Drag Artivists in the South

Freedom Tunnel Press

IT'S SOULFUL AND IT'S SURVIVAL

A Conversation with Four Drag Artivists in the South

OSO CHANEL   LOLITA CHANEL   NOVA STELLA   ONYA NERVES

EDITED BY BROOKE SHAFFNER
DESIGNED BY NITEESH ELIAS

INTRODUCTION

.

I grew up in the mid-90s, cheering on a drag queen friend in my small Texas-Mexico bordertown's only gay bar. Witnessing the transfiguration of drag, I understood what it was to be an artist—to throw open the borders of the known world. Though it was long before I realized I was queer, I felt free and embraced in that space. That experience inspired my novel *Country of Under*, about the transformative friendship between two intelligent, misfit young people carving out their place in the world, in their small Texican town and later in New York City.

Fast-forward to 2022. After 20 years in NYC, I was ready for a change. My partner Niteesh had an opportunity to transfer to Charlotte, North Carolina, so we traveled there. During his lunch break on his first visit to the Charlotte office, he met Derek Kramer/Onya Nerves, who was soon to leave a career in real estate to found the drag collective DKO Entertainment. That weekend, we went to a drag bingo hosted by Onya Nerves and watched Oso Chanel, a Salvadoran-American drag king, perform to Selena, whose death had devastated my high school. It felt like home and some magic all Oso's own.

Niteesh and I have now lived in Charlotte for a year and a half, during which we've enjoyed many drag shows and watched our favorite drag performers ascend to new leadership platforms.

As the first immigrant crowned Mr. Charlotte Pride, Oso Chanel (he/him) is focused on decriminalizing immigrants and helping LGBTQIA+ immigrants to access health resources.

As National MX, Nova Stella (they/them) is focused on HIV advocacy, prevention, and care. They are an Executive Assistant at Dudley's Place, which serves individuals living with or at risk for HIV in the Charlotte area.

As the first Latine person to win Mx Charlotte Pride, Lolita Chanel (they/them) is focused on bringing drag to underserved smaller cities and being a beacon of Pride, body positivity, and love.

As the founder of DKO Entertainment, Onya Nerves (she/they) strives to create safe spaces for new drag entertainers to grow and thrive, especially POC and trans performers.

Amid the rise of drag bans and anti-queer legislation and attacks, performing drag *is* activism. But these four performers also advocate for immigrants, HIV care, body positivity, POC performers, and performers who live with disabilities. They create small-town Pride celebrations and fight drag bans at city council meetings, urge their audiences to vote, and organize boycotts against racist bars. They create drag that breaks the mold, enlarging the space for queerness, for all of us.

This project began as a brief interview for *Scoundrel Time* and turned into a four-hour conversation in which Oso, Lolita, Nova, and Onya discussed the issues they're focused on and the power of drag to create social change. Listening to them talk about facing down death threats and protests, on top of drag bans and anti-queer and trans bills, and the unique power of drag in the South, which they describe as being about survival and the creation of queer history, felt like a revolution in our living room. In the wake of great danger, these artivists continue to make and change history. We've recorded their voices here because we believe that they are vital to our queer history and our collective movement forward.

HOW DID EACH OF YOU COME TO DRAG?

Brooke: How did each of you come to drag?

Jaime/Oso: I came to drag through Lolita. I had moved from New York in 2006 to Graham, North Carolina, which is very rural, very white. Once I graduated high school, I told my parents, "I love you guys, but I can't grow here. There's no space for me here." I came down to Charlotte and I went to Scorpio[1]. It was my first interaction with anything queer related, drag related. I saw Angela Lopez, Brooklyn Dior, Felicia Monet. That was my first introduction to drag overall, but I got into doing drag through Lolita. We became friends because—

Sebastian/Lolita: begrudgingly (laughs)

Brooke: You were rivals first? (laughs)

Jaime/Oso: When we first met at Scorpio, I think I, like, shook their hand and that was it. I was a very different person back then. But once we started becoming friends, I think I was the one who was like, "Do you want to come over and paint my face?"

Sebastian/Lolita: The first day we hung out, I had a trip to Mexico the next day, but I got off work early, so when Oso invited me over, I thought, Might as well. After hanging out for a bit, he was like, "I've never had anyone do my makeup before." I was like, "Do you want to?" So I drove back to my house, picked up my makeup, came back, did their makeup and he was like obsessed with it even though it was really bad. And yeah, that was kind of how things went from there.

Jaime/Oso: And then a couple of days after their trip back, Sebastian came over. I sat in my bathroom on my toilet watching them turn from Sebastian

---

1   The Scorpio was Charlotte's longest running LGBTQ+ nightclub, which opened in 1968 and closed on October 31st, 2023.

into Lolita, seeing the transformation, and then I became their dresser. So I saw things from backstage. I saw, instead of the makeup transformation, the physical transformation from Sebastian to Lolita. So that was how I got introduced to drag—through Lolita.

Brooke: Both you and Lolita have your own amazing versions of drag. Oso, you, especially, are breaking down all kinds of boundaries. I'm wondering how you came to your version of what a drag king is?

Jaime/Oso: I spent almost four years being Lolita's dresser, so I saw a big variety of what drag was. 90% of it was drag queens.

Derek/Onya: All of it was versions of what we do. (Everyone laughs.)

Sebastian/Lolita: You're not wrong.

Jaime/Oso: I would hear Lolita be like, "Oh my God, I would love to be like Nina Fierra, I would love to be like Carrie Chanel," who were staple drag queens in Charlotte. But there was really no one that I could look up to, because there was no brown king, there was no Latine king, there was no plus-sized Latine king or male lead. So when I got into drag, I had a conversation with Lolita and Carrie Chanel, her drag mother, and Carrie told me, "Go out there and be that person, that entertainer that you want to look up to," so that's where I get a lot of my drive for drag. I want to be the drag role model that I needed when I was younger because there wasn't anybody that looked like me. There wasn't anybody that performed the music, you know, the rhythms, the cultural things. Of course, there was Nina Fierra, Angela Lopez, and Kassandra Hylton, but they were all queens, and I never saw myself truly being a drag queen.

Brooke: The first time I saw you perform, Niteesh and I had come down from New York to check out Charlotte and decide whether we wanted move here. Andrew[2] took us to drag bingo—

---

2   Andrew Williams, a designer whom Niteesh briefly managed at Honeywell, who is now a dear friend, connected us to Derek, Jaime, Logan, and Sebastian.

Jaime/Oso: At Resident Culture[3], I remember (laughs)

Brooke: And you performed to Selena, who was huge where I grew up. When Selena died, my whole high school mourned. So you performing Selena was amazing. It felt like home.

Derek/Onya: So how I got introduced to drag…. I've always kind of been on my own. I've never really had a mentor above me. My drag mom now, she's just a mom, she doesn't know what she's doing. And I love her to death. She's a sweetheart and she's more there for advice, but I got my start in drag in college. Wildly enough, I was the first openly gay person to join my fraternity. Most of them became president of our fraternity and then came out because they couldn't be—

Logan/Nova: How was that hazing?

Derek/Onya: SigEp does not haze.

Brooke: SigEp guys were the nice guys at Davidson.

Derek/Onya: They usually are. Nerdy, very nerdy. But yeah, that resounds from all chapters, which is kind of nice. SDSU (South Dakota State University) has a pageant called Miss Homelycoming[4]. Because I was the first openly out one, me and my friend, Nick, who was a performer from the Bay Area who somehow got roped into moving from San Francisco to South Dakota, were like, Okay, so Miss Homelycoming is coming up. Let's do it. I did it because my fraternity got points for competing. If I won, they got lots of points. So if we were going to do it, we were going to do it to the nines. We went out and bought outfits for our presentation and our gown and our talent, all that stuff. Miss Homelycoming is mostly known for farmer bros going to Goodwill, getting whatever dress fits, and just doing it "guy in a dress". Because of that, the contestants had to go before

---

3 Resident Culture Brewery in Plaza Midwood

4 South Dakota State's Miss Homelycoming pageant was a yearly event during Homecoming week in which 8-15 men dressed as women and competed in swimwear, eveningwear, talent, and interview skills. The winner of Miss Homelycoming rode in the Hobo Day parade and was asked to help with fund raisers and make appearances in full garb. The Miss Homelycoming pageant began in 2006. Derek/Onya competed in 2010 and 2011. It's unclear whether it still happens. The last online record I can find is for 2016.

a panel in their outfits two days before the pageant to get approval. They didn't want a guy walking up on stage with his ass hanging out, so the panel would say, "Well, this doesn't fit you, so you need to find something else." Me and Nick showed up to the panel in full head-to-toe drag. Madison McQueen was Nick's performer name. All the other boys were like, Oh, this is SERIOUS. So we all showed up on Wednesday, two days later, and every single one of the contestants had drag moms from other sororities. They were all dressed to the nines, well, as much as straight men in dresses can be—

Sebastian/Lolita: I was gonna say. (Everyone laughs.)

Derek/Onya: For South Dakota, Miss Homelycoming was pretty good for the first year—2006. But every year since Nick and I performed in 2010, the pageant has stayed at the same high level. I got to help start that. But that was my first foray into drag, and then it was probably a good eight years after that I basically had accumulated enough outfits from Halloween, little group events, and fundraisers that I decided I had way too much invested to not be utilizing it. And so then I started performing.

Jaime/Oso: What was that pageant outfit like? What did you wear?

Derek/Onya: Oh, it was god awful. It was so bad. We were all obsessed with Lady Gaga. And back then I was literally half the size I am now. Like I was a meager 160 pounds. I was tiny and tall. It was gross. Adderall is a hell of a drug. Prescribed. So I was in three different Lady Gaga outfits and Halloween costumes because it was in October. And it was so bad.

Brooke: But it was the first time.

Derek/Onya: It was the first time, of course. Like I didn't cover my eyebrows. I still don't cover my eyebrows. Things are the same. (Everyone laughs.)

Sebastian/Lolita: The frequency is the only thing that's changed. (Everyone laughs.)

Derek/Onya: The frequency that I put on makeup has increased exponentially, but I still wore giant heels for Miss Homelycoming because I've always had big feet, so you're not gonna find a small heel. But yeah, then I moved down from college to Charlotte and got started with Stonewall Sports[5]. Once a season, they did a charity fundraiser for the nonprofits they were under at the time. So we'd perform in our groups and raise all this money.

Brooke: You're often raising money for good causes or folks in your community who are struggling. So drag for you has long been intertwined with raising money for charities?

Derek/Onya: Always. Everything has always been some sort of a fundraiser or benefit for something.

Sebastian/Lolita: That's the only tax write-off she gets. (Derek laughs.)

So I hate to be the stereotypical one here, but my introduction to drag was Drag Race. It was back when it was on Netflix.

Jaime/Oso: Oh, season one, season two! (laughter)

Sebastian/Lolita: Season one wasn't allowed to be on Netflix. It was the lost season because they were trying to scrub it off the internet and the gays said no. I watched season two and season three of Drag Race on Netflix. I grew up with a best friend, Mark. We started watching Drag Race when we were 15, 16 years old. The only experience I'd had with drag before that was a friend's birthday party where they had a drag queen. But I was so deep and heavily into the closet then that I stood at the bar and turned away. I was very uncomfortable the whole time. Besides the birthday boy, I was the only other openly queer person. So they were all like, "Oh, that's going to be you one year." You know, like, kind of right. But at 16, I watched Drag Race with my best friend and we started having commentary, like, Why'd she wear that outfit? Why'd she do that? She could have done that, she should've done this. Or, they're not giving a lot of energy, they should be dancing more, whatever.

Little by little, we started dipping our toes into buying dresses and heels and Amazon wigs. We eventually got into this nonprofit here in Charlotte called TOY

---

5   Stonewall Sports is the largest LGBTQ+ sports organization in the Carolinas.

(Time Out Youth[6]). They had these days where they brought clothes for trans kids to rummage through and see what they wanted. Even though I was not homeless or anything, I still went in there and found dresses I liked. I didn't take anything home for a long time because I was scared of my parents ever finding dresses, but little by little, I started buying some things.

Then one day, a group of drag queens went into TOY because they were getting ready to protest. And that's how I met my first drag mother, Vegas Van Dank. From there, I started going to gay bars and clubs.

Brooke: What were you protesting?

Sebastian/Lolita: This was, I want to say, 2012, 2013. So it was it was right around the era where we were starting the movement for marriage equality if I'm not mistaken.

Brooke: Right, gay marriage was legalized in 2015.

Sebastian/Lolita: So we were making protest posters, but I was asking them [Vegas Van Dank] a million questions about performing and going on stage, like how does it feel with your wig on. So eventually me and my best friend started performing together. They unfortunately stopped. They went by the name of Abortia Clinic. (Laughs) Yeah, a very heavy name. I've always been Lolita, but my last name has changed a few times. We're not gonna go into the history of that, but…

(laughter and comments from the drag entertainers)

Sebastian/Lolita: Shut up (laughing).

Jaime/Oso: Document it, document it.

Sebastian/Lolita: Oh my god.

---

6   Time Out Youth is a nonprofit where LGBTQ+ youth ages 13-24 can experience a sense of belonging and community.

Brooke: You're House of Chanel now with Oso. Did you all create your own house?

Sebastian/Lolita: Kind of. We helped create it, I would say. Our drag grandmother is Elaine Davis. She doesn't have the family name, but she was kind of the motivation, the person who helped—

(Oso gives Lolita a look.)

Sebastian/Lolita: I know, there's history there. But she's the one who kind of helps our drag mother Carrie Chanel. I originally asked Carrie Chanel to be my drag mother and she was like, I'm not looking to have kids. It's not for me, whatever.

Brooke: Is it a lot of responsibility?

Sebastian/Lolita: Oh, truly it is. Especially nowadays, you're basically co-signing everything that person does. So you have to be really comfortable with that person.

Brooke (to Onya): But you have many children.

Derek/Onya: Um-hum, unfortunately, so many kids.

Jaime/Oso: Nova has zero.

Logan/Nova: Unofficially, like one. Art.

Brooke: It's okay to be child-free. (Everyone laughs.)

Sebastian/Lolita: Well, I mean, the blind leading the blind is always helpful, but anyways—

(Oso, who was mentored by Lolita, laughs, and Lolita says, "I love you so much.")

Sebastian/Lolita: Regarding Carrie (Chanel), I had gotten to a place in my drag where I was performing in a very different style from my previous house, House of Terror. They're more focused on alternative and unconventional performances, versus I was someone who heavily appreciated the drag pageant history and a lot of the legends in Charlotte. I was kind of a history nerd. My drag was starting to change more into that. And then, I fell out with my house drag mother. I mean, we're good now. But back then we really fell out. I remember one night I was leaving the bar and Carrie cornered me for a second. She asked, "Are you really looking to leave your house?" I said, "Yes." She said, "Okay, as of today, you are now Lolita Chanel. You have given us a lot of things and you have been able to let go of a lot of things. I love you, go home and get some rest." I didn't sleep at all because I was so happy.

Brooke: So the house mother sort of determines your aesthetic, or it's a dialogue, a collaboration?

Sebastian/Lolita: I would say more a collaboration because—how would I put it—I was always encouraged to do spookier things when I was under Vegas. And that's perfectly fine. To some people, that is their artistic expression, that's where they feel the most comfortable. But I didn't always feel super connected to it. And then with Carrie, Carrie has always been more on the pageant side, the more pretty, typical side of drag, I guess you could say. Under her, I feel like my drag has grown exponentially. I have achieved new heights that I couldn't have reached before. Also, back then my name was Lolita Van Dank. The "Van Dank" wasn't as family friendly as Lolita Chanel. Lolita Chanel's a little friendlier to people.

Logan/Nova: For me, how I came to drag... In high school, I fell in love with theater arts. I had always had different hobbies. I played piano and clarinet and showed horses. My hobbies were all over the place, but then in high school, I really found my passion for theater arts because my favorite teacher started a theater arts class my sophomore year. Because I loved her from my English class, I said, Oh, I'm going to take her theatre arts course. I had done plays at church and Christmas pageants, but I really fell in love with theater arts in high school. I had planned on going to college for law. Every single year, from the summer after eighth grade to the summer after 11th grade, I went to a 3-week law course in Nashville, Tennessee. And it was after my junior year that I was like, I'm not going to do this. I see how miserable my father is. I'm not gonna do this myself and I went against everything my parents were saying and decided to go to school for theater.

Well, when I got out of school, I acknowledged the fact that it was really hard to find work in small-town Tennessee in theater. The only way that I would have been able to get a job was if I went to the Gatlinburg area, but it wasn't really doing what I wanted to do. That would have been more, like, shows for tourists, not live theater as I see it, you know, Broadway and plays and musicals. So I started working full time at Ulta Beauty because it was new in the town that I was living in and I fell in love with beauty makeup. I had already done special effects makeup with a haunted house that I worked at seasonally. And of course, I knew stage makeup from theater. But because I was working full time, it was hard to find time for rehearsals for local community theater productions. So I fell out of the theater scene. Then I met my—I call him my brother—my friend Hunter. Hunter had started performing drag in the fall of 2017 in a place in Sevierville, Tennessee called the Glow Sky Lounge. A friend who'd grown up around Hunter in the tattoo shops connected us. She was like, "Oh my God, you need to meet him. He's started doing drag. I think you all would get along." So she introduced us, and we started hanging out. Fast forward to February of 2018: Hunter kept dropping hints, saying, "Oh, you should do drag sometime." And I was like, Oh, I could never, like I wouldn't, that's not for me, I can't do that. I had been watching Ru Paul's Drag Race because it piqued my interest and I binge-watched from, like, season four to that time, I think it was season nine. I had been sneaking out to the gay bar, even though I was straight—dating a girl. I had been sneaking out to get a feel of what the scene was like, if that was really what my life was leading me to.

[A beat of silence, and then everyone bursts into laughter]

Derek/Onya: We're learning so much about each other!

Logan/Nova: I know, I dated a girl for two and a half years.

Sebastian/Lolita: This whole time I had to hold back. I was like, Girl, she didn't know?

Logan/Nova: She did not, bless her heart. However, I started sneaking out to the shows and I was secretly falling in love with drag. It was amazing because it was theater. It was the transformation, seeing the entertainers do a different act in every single performance, because I grew up in the era of true southern pageant drag where you have a different costume, different hair, different shoes. It was just amazing watching them transform themselves within 10 minutes to come out there and do another performance that was completely different than what they did before. So, February 2018, I think I got a text message on February 27th, and it was like 3 pm in the afternoon, it was a Tuesday and Hunter texted me. He said, "Hey, I've had two people drop out of the show tomorrow night. There's only two of us. We typically have six of us. Some people just can't be there." Two had dropped out because of whatever they had come up. "You should come out and perform." And I was like, you're giving me a day's notice? That's not gonna work. He said, "You can use my wigs. You know, I'm bigger than you, so I don't really have costumes you can use." I wear size seven and a half, eight in men's shoes. He was like, "You absolutely can't use my shoes because it'll be like walking in your mama's shoes when you're three-years-old." So I called my best friend Brooke, and I was like, "Um, I need help. They're putting me in a drag show tomorrow and I didn't say no." And she was like, "A day's notice?! We can't come up with something—" So we went shopping. We went to Forever 21. We went to Torrid. I mean, we went to all these different places.

Sebastian/Lolita: laughs.

Logan/Nova: What?

Sebastian/Lolita: No, when I started performing, I also went to Torrid. But I'm also fat.

Sebastian/Lolita: So am I. Torrid's great. We were shopping and trying to make things come together. We could not find a look. I didn't know what I wanted to go for. I had not thought out a name. I had not come up with a persona. And I ended up just raiding Brooke's and her sister's closet. I borrowed shoes from her. Hunter let me borrow some wigs. My favorite color at the time was this purple-blue, like a periwinkle color. And we're sitting around Brooke's, my best friend's, dining room table. I'm trying to do my makeup, eyebrows at my hairline (everyone laughs) and eye shadow bled completely into my eyebrows. It was horrendous, but we're sitting there and she's like, "Well, what are they gonna announce you as, like what's your name going to be?" And I was like, "Oh god, I really don't know." We were throwing names around. At the time, I was listening a lot to Little Mix and my favorite member of Little Mix was Perrie. I was like, I could go by my middle name, because my middle name is Perry. Oh wait. What if I did a campy-funny type persona and called myself Periwinkle because it's my favorite color? And that's what I was for the first three months of performing.

It wasn't until I started trying to get serious that I took Hunter's name. I took the name Nova Majors at the time because his name was Nebula Majors. It wasn't until we disbanded the family that I was like, Okay, well I have to find a new last name now. I went on Google and was finding names that were associated with Nova, and one that kept popping up was Stella Nova, which means bright star. And I was like, Oh, what a testament to me as a person, I try to be a bright light in everybody's life, I try to be the bright star, so flip it and make it Nova Stella. And here we are six years later.

WHAT EXCITES YOU MOST ABOUT DRAG AS AN ART FORM?

Brooke: What excites you most about drag as an art form?

Logan/Nova: The transformation of who the person is, before and after getting into drag, and the passion when someone pours their heart out and commands the room.

Derek/Onya: The possibilities. When I started producing shows, my thing was drag in unusual places. I like to push the envelope of what people think is acceptable or where we can do shows, where we can be visible as queer people. This year, I've gotten into full Broadway productions. I don't have time to audition for plays, but with drag, I can produce my own play, perform whatever part I want, and make drag an even bigger part of the art, which is what I really like, because people get so pigeonholed in what they think they can or can't do.

Jaime/Oso: What excites me most is the storytelling and the act of recording of queer history. Because we're posting our pictures on Facebook. People are tagging us in their stories on Instagram, Facebook, and Snapchat. I love listening to other people's stories. Truly, genuinely. The active recording of queer history, because queer history—there's not one specific way. There are so many different ways to define what being queer is, and I think through our art form, and individually, we all bring so many different things that we're recording. That way, two, three generations down the road, they won't have to deal with the things that we're dealing with. We'll be able to be a small part of that change.

Logan/Nova: We truly have the opportunity to rewrite the future for the people who come after us.

Sebastian/Lolita: For so long, queer history has been such a hush-hush topic, something that was pushed away, that by demanding to be taken seriously, and also taken as offering value, we are changing history. What excites me most about drag is its power to impact people. In 2016, 2017, AFAB (Assigned Female at Birth) people doing drag as hyper-feminine people was a very hot topic. They were not seen as taking drag seriously—the whole, "Oh, yeah, it's gonna be really easy for you because you don't have to go through the same things that we do." And that's not the case. One of those performers said something that, to this day, stuck with me: "Drag is the power of commanding the space that you're in." I want to be something that, in my everyday life, I don't know if I have the same power to be. But in drag, I can walk on stage in my outfit and catch everyone's eye. In that moment, it's irresistible for someone to look at you. That, to me, is what I love: the impact that I have on people, or just commanding that space.

Brooke: I wanted you to end my book launch with "Because the Night" because you make people cry with your soulful ballads.

Sebastian/Lolita: When I do a ballad, I'm doing it from a place of hurt. Something that's hurting me is what I bring on stage. I want everyone in the crowd to feel what I'm feeling. Sometimes someone tries to do a number that's very emotionally charged and it doesn't quite carry the same tune because they're not really sharing their story, they're sharing their sob story. I've been attacked mercilessly online, along with most of us here, and I have a number dedicated to certain Christians who've targeted us and made us out to be these evil people. I have another number that I call my "Big Girl Mix". It's a spoken word number that moves into song, where I'm talking about what it's like for a plus-sized person, specifically a plus-sized woman, to go to a doctor and be dismissed, like, "Oh, you're not really sick. You're just fat." It's a way to convey the message that I have faced this, and I know someone else has also faced this. So, take this moment to find connection with someone who's had similar experiences.

One of my favorite things about the more emotional numbers I do is that, in that moment, I can provide some kind of comfort. I don't know who you are or your story, but if I see that what I'm saying or what I'm bringing to the stage is very impactful, I'm not ashamed to kneel down and hug someone. Sometimes the whole number, all I'm doing is hugging people and letting them have a moment to let it all out.

TELL ME ABOUT THE ORIGIN OF AND MOTIVATION BEHIND YOUR ACTIVISM.

Brooke: Tell me about the origin of and motivation behind your activism.

Logan/Nova: Silence. Silence for so long. I was taught by my family, who are extremely conservative and Republican, that silence was the only way to go. If you did not agree with people, if you had differing opinions: silence. They didn't want the conflict. They did not want the discourse in the family. So, when I found my footing as a drag entertainer and found out what it truly meant to be at the forefront of our queer community and the politics that come with that, the silence of my childhood and not really agreeing with how I was raised and the politics in the area where I was raised, that's what really drove me to activism and speaking out against the things I disagree with.

Derek/Onya: My mother's motto was, "If you're not helping, you're hurting." Growing up, I saw her advocate for domestic violence victims and take care of children who didn't have the necessities to live day to day. There was never a day growing up that we did not have at least 13 or 14 kids running around the yard. And snack time was always the same. Everyone knew that if their child wasn't at their house, they were at ours. And it just so happened that a lot of the kids were from very low-income families. So my advocacy started with that. I always want to help however I can, sometimes to a fault. Everyone needs a little help sometimes.

Jaime/Oso: For me, the origin is being an immigrant and a child of immigrants. My parents came to this country for a better future for me and my siblings. But I don't think I've reached that better future. Back then, there was no social media, no real internet. So, you would hear from people who crossed borders to come to the US and wrote letters back that money grew on trees; it was truly the American dream. I think now, that American dream for immigrants, especially from Latin America, is more of an American sacrifice. I acknowledge that my life would be totally different had I stayed in El Salvador. I wouldn't be here in this room with you. I wouldn't be here. I'd probably be dead because in El Salvador back then, being queer, trans was a death sentence, and it still is in some parts. But I think what drives my activism is that I'm still searching for that better future. There are times when I am out in public and I can pass for straight, which is a privilege, but if I can live a day where I don't need to pass as a self-defense, I'm getting closer to that better future that my parents wanted.

Of course, I'm the first one in both my parents' families to graduate high school. I didn't go to college because we weren't educated about the application process. In New York at that time, I could not go to college. I was too old when DACA started. I think you had to be under eight when the program got introduced by Obama. Our family had to find a different path. I'm a legal resident now—still can't vote—but I use that to educate people. A lot of people are surprised that I can't vote. The first time I spoke about it in Monroe, I had a panic attack in the back afterwards because I was standing in front of a room of majority white people who would never have thought, after seeing an amazing performance, that the performer couldn't vote. I'm still searching for the better life that my parents sacrificed so much to give me and that's what I use to motivate myself.

Sebastian/Lolita: My motivation is similar to Oso's, being that we're both Latine, with parents who came to this country because they bought the fantasy of the American dream. I'm motivated by seeing what my parents, family, and the people I grew up with had to show up through, like the constant fear of being stopped by the police, the constant fear when every day in this country was a gift because the next one they could be found and sent back, and if they were sent back, they were going to be killed, because if you made the journey to America and returned to Chile, you were seen as a traitor and they killed you. For a long time, Chile was under a dictatorship by Pinochet. I lost an uncle because of him. He was very involved in activism and spoke out about how things were not okay in Chile. He came to this country for a little bit, was quickly found by immigration, and was sent back. Two days later, the military squad killed him. No investigation or anything. If you're found by immigration and sent back, if you have any life at all, you're not going to have a good one. The reason I try so hard to be an activist, even though I'm a citizen because I was born here, is that I see my family and friends struggling and not having the same power. Like I often say at shows, my grandmother has lived in this country for 50 years and cannot vote.

Brooke: There's no path for her?

Sebastian/Lolita: It's not that there's no path, it's that it is a very expensive path. To become a citizen, it would cost, I want to say, anywhere between $1,200 and $2,000. That's just for an application, that's not even a guarantee that you get citizenship. That's a whole separate process.

Jaime/Oso: A lot of places provide waivers for your residency status or citizenship, but there are so many hurdles. You have to make less than a certain amount and it's a very unconventional amount. A lot of people who have a resident status cannot have a social security number, which makes it even more difficult when it comes to tax returns and getting paid.

Sebastian/Lolita: Not having to know the cost or understand the process of becoming a citizen of this country is a privilege. Because of those privileges, I want to be a voice for people who cannot speak for themselves, people who are afraid to speak for themselves. There's such a fear in the Latine community of being caught by the police if you're undocumented, and even sometimes if you are documented. While I have the privilege of citizenship, I'm going to make sure that their stories are told, that their voices are heard, and that I can speak for them. That's why I always make speeches saying, "If you don't feel like voting, vote for my family, friends, and neighbors who can't because they are not seen as humans in this country."

Jaime/Oso: These parents were protesting an immigration ruling and they had duct tape over their mouths and their sign read, "Dear son, Thank you for screaming out loud what we have silenced for years." Our immigrant parents, because they don't know the law and the language, because of all these barriers, they tend to be silent about a lot of things. I have conversations with my parents all the time and they're, like, "We're proud that you're doing all these things, but please be safe," because the more vocal I am, especially as someone who is documented but unable to vote, all it's going to take is for somebody to call ICE. They know my government name, and especially now with how the immigration system is, not only is it expensive, but it's extremely difficult because any interaction with law enforcement is a flag through the process.

Still, I think, as children of immigrants, we are the ones to resist because Lolita's family couldn't do that back in Chile. My family couldn't do that because I was born at the end of a civil war in El Salvador, because of the tactics used to contain communism. So, I think it's very important for us to continue to be vocal, to be loud, regardless of whether it makes other people, specifically our white counterparts, uncomfortable because they have a privilege that—. There's so much noise and a lot of our voices are being silenced. But we have to continue to be loud. There's no other way. Because we've tried. We've tried being patient. We've tried to sign the petitions. And then we get arrested for protesting, but there's no other way than to shake the system in the way that it needs to be shaken, to either find a path to fix it, or to just completely start over.

WHAT ISSUES DO YOU WANT TO ADDRESS AS LEADERS IN THE QUEER COMMUNITY?

Brooke: You've all recently ascended to new leadership platforms and/or been recognized as leaders in the community. Congratulations! What issues do you want to address in these leadership positions, particularly as we approach an election year? How do you see these issues as intertwined with your drag artistry?

Jaime/Oso: In 2015, I started volunteering with Charlotte Pride. I built the foundation for Charlotte Latin pride. But one of the things that I'm extremely excited about is to rebuild and relaunch it. Charlotte Pride made the decision to switch it from Charlotte Latinx Pride to Charlotte Latine Pride.

Logan/Nova: Are both Latinx and Latine considered gender inclusive umbrella terms? What's the preference there?

Jaime/Oso: Latine has been commonly used in Latin America. In the Spanish language, there aren't a lot of words that end in "x". So Latinx in Spanish doesn't really flow, nor does it exist. Latinx was a word coined here in America.

Logan/Nova: And probably anglicized.

Jaime/Oso: Yeah. So Latine flows with the language.

Logan/Nova: It originated with the culture. It's not coined by Caucasians.

Sebastian/Lolita: Also, it does make it easier on the language. [Demonstrates how to use "Latine" in Spanish.] It flows more with conversation.

Logan/Nova: If you were to say Latinx, it's almost like a harsh stop.

Jaime/Oso: Spanish is a gendered language. It's a romance language. Using "Latine" is a way to not break with tradition and custom, but still try to keep it as non-binary as possible. So we're branding and creating the logo for Charlotte Latine Pride. But the performance you saw me do at Pride [Oso powerfully took on the criminalization of immigrants with a dramatic narrative performance to "Stand Up" by Cynthia Erivo], I want to bring more awareness to that—the criminalization of immigrants—from my platform because it's something that's very, very dear to my heart. Because art, music, reading, writing, anything art-related is so embedded in Latine culture. I can be in a room of people that I don't know, but all it's gonna take is that one song for us to get up and start dancing, and I think music and arts are just ways of bringing people together. So I want to bring more visibility to that. I also want to bring more visibility to the lack of POC entertainers and kings and things in more traditional, mainstream shows— not just locally, but Drag Race has, what, 16 seasons now, and all these franchises around the world. They had All Stars and all these things. Metamorphosis was the first straight man. Gottmik, if I'm not mistaken, was the first trans man. It took forever to acknowledge and allow trans women and it's been 16 seasons, so let's say 20 years of Drag Race here in the US, right? There hasn't been a king on Drag Race. Other than Dragula, I don't think there's another nationally watched drag competition show.

Derek/Onya: That [Dragula] still is low-grade.

Jaime/Oso: I think that, in a way, Drag Race helped mainstream drag queens and I think I stand by that firmly because when people have never been to a drag show— Last night, there was a—I believe they were a couple from England—they were doing a paper on drag in America here. They had never been to a drag show. They didn't know what a king was.

Brooke: Well, when I first experienced kings, it was butch lesbians performing in masculine dress, so you were a totally new iteration of "king" to me. I was like, This is amazing.

Jaime/Oso: Most assigned male at birth people who do drag as male entertainers are traditionally called "male leads." Drag kings normally identify as female outside of drag, but in drag, they are male-impersonating or male-presenting. With me, my makeup never fit traditional male lead, my costumes never fit traditional male lead, my numbers never fit traditional male either. I had a conversation with the king community because I didn't want to overstep and take spotlight.

They accepted me 100%, and I think I'm trying my best to acknowledge the fact that, as a cis man performing as a drag king, I have a lot of privileges, but to use those privileges to showcase a diverse cast, which Onya does an amazing job of. Having kings, having things, and just more variety because the more people are seeing drag, it's extremely important for them to see all forms of drag because you never know who's in the crowd wanting to start performing, and I don't want them to feel like me 10 years ago when I had no one to look up to. I want them to be able to see someone on that stage and say, Oh my god, they look like me. Their performance is an experience that I have also gone through.

Brooke: What does a traditional male lead look like typically? What do you mean when you say that your makeup, costumes, and numbers never fit traditional male lead?

Logan/Nova: A lot of male leads don't wear a lot of makeup.

Derek/Onya: They'll wear foundation if anything, and that's pretty much it.

Logan/Nova: They give the "Ken doll look". That's what I always called it, the "Ken doll look". One of the male leads I know in Texas is literally called Ken Doll.

Jaime/Oso: I think, traditionally, male leads will only do male-sung songs. Or their performances will—

Derek/Onya: crucify a female song and auto-tune it to a male one. At least that's what happens a lot of the time.

Jaime/Oso: That's not to take away from male leads. I think it's just acknowledging the fact that not all drag queens are gay men in dresses, but that not all male entertainers are male leads or kings, to be able to have a uniform term, but at the same time acknowledge that under that umbrella, there are so many subforms of male lead and drag king. I'm pretty sure that there are entertainers who aren't male leads or kings, who are creating their own category.

Derek/Onya: The issues I want to address are very similar to what Oso said. Visibility above all else is my main goal for next year, especially in Charlotte. There are ebbs and flows in every area, but supporting the growth of the baby queens and kings and things is important because we are losing our queer spaces at such a rapid pace. There's not really a safe place for a lot of these newer entertainers to come out and grow and be allowed to fail. Chasers[1] used to host a talent show every Wednesday back in the day. You would show up with your CD or flash drive. You had to be there by a certain time. The first eight, or however many, people got to compete. I don't know if there was ever really a limit or they just said that. And then at the end of the night, you either won or you lost, and if you won, you got to come back the next month with a paid booking. There's just not that kind of environment anymore.

Brooke: That's how my drag advisor for Country of Under got started, through a talent show: "10-minute slot, show us what you got!"

Derek/Onya: I didn't personally do the talent shows when I was coming up.

Sebastian/Lolita: (to Oso) You didn't start through the talent shows.

Jaime/Oso: I didn't, but I also had a strong drag foundation and a lot of experience.

Logan/Nova: This day five years ago was the first time I ever won a talent contest.

Derek/Onya: One thing we've discussed a lot over the last couple of months is the lack of representation of POC and Latine performers. We even sat down one night and made a list so that we knew who to call on to make sure that our shows aren't stagnant. For how I do things, I want to include a trans performer, a POC performer, a Latine performer... to showcase as diverse a range of performers as possible within budget restrictions. I also want to create spaces where they can grow and flourish that aren't... overpowering is the way I want to say it, very white, in very white areas. That's just something that can be very off-putting for someone who is coming up in the world of drag and then shows up to a talent show and it's just every white queen and king and they're the only Latine or POC

1   https://www.chaserscharlotte.com/

person. That can be very off-putting and feel unwelcoming. Whether it is or not, that's how it's going to be perceived.

I just want to be able to create diverse, welcoming, inclusive spaces in the next year to five years. It's not gonna be an overnight thing—no matter how we always answer our pageant questions. It's a long process and it's something that Charlotte has been struggling with for decades.

Jaime/Oso: I think it's also off-putting for non-English-speaking people, not just Spanish speakers but also people who speak other languages, to have no way to communicate with a show director or a venue or even feel comfortable, because maybe they don't listen to English music. Maybe they only speak French and they love, let's say, this French artist. How would you bridge that?

Derek/Onya: A couple of my friends in Atlanta have started incorporating ASL into their shows. That's a huge thing. Growing up in South Dakota, we had a school for the deaf nearby. Ironically, every deaf person I met in South Dakota was gay, which I don't know if there's something for later... (Everyone laughs)

But they had to travel in their own group and weren't really able to go out enjoy the drag shows back home—the one night a month that they would happen. My friends in Atlanta have had really good success incorporating ASL into their shows. I've tried to do it up here a few times, but either the show gets canceled because of a lack of interest or we're unable to afford an interpreter.

While we might have our own internal disabilities, it's very easy not to actively think about other people's disabilities and what they're capable of, or what might prevent them from enjoying a show. I want to create an even more inclusive experience because if people in the audience are not enjoying or not able to experience the full show, they're not going to come back, and we don't want that to happen.

Brooke: In Brooklyn, the performances in the park, Celebrate Brooklyn, always had ASL interpreters and it was a beautiful thing to watch. The way that they interpreted music and dance was its own artform.

Derek/Onya: I've talked to a few ASL interpreters down here who would be willing to donate their time, or there are grants that I could apply for to get assistance, or pro bono stuff, but the reason why you don't see a lot of ASL interpreters is because it takes a lot of time to prepare for a show. They need drag performers to give them the songs a week in advance because they have to think deeply about how to translate a song. Not every word in a song is going to be easily translated into ASL, or they might have to look up a combination that encompasses a phrase. There's a lot of research that interpreters do, so they're very worth their time. But drag performers are very last minute. Either we're processing x,y, and z shows a week, so we're not able to think a week in advance about which songs we want to perform. Or we just don't have the budget. A lot of our shows, we're working on $200 for a whole show, and that's to pay a DJ, hosts, and the performers. Usually, one person does five or six things.

Sebastian/Lolita: Which is Onya.

Derek/Onya: It's me, yeah.

Sebastian/Lolita: We love her so much.

Derek/Onya: Hours and hours of dedication go into creating a show that runs smoothly and looks flawless. If you see a hiccup, that means you also didn't see the 65 others that could have happened during that same event.

Sebastian/Lolita: Oh my god, just today with the music.

Jaime/Oso: Lolita and I recently got the chance to perform in DC and we had to send our lyrics a week before the show so that the interpreter could memorize the lyrics. Then the night of, it was really cool because we got to meet the interpreters and ask them questions. I don't know ASL—

Sebastian/Lolita: I know a little ASL.

Jaime/Oso: But it was really fun to look back at the videos. One of our performances projected body positivity and another was about insecurity, and the ASL interpreters were emoting just like us entertainers. There are specific ways that they communicate emotion and energy, like you said. An ASL interpreter at a concert is going to be a little more high-energy with their hand movements. Looking back at clips from Charlotte Pride, I realized that an ASL interpreter was signing throughout our performances, but the entire time I was performing, to be honest with you, I never even saw it.

Sebastian/Lolita: Going back to what Onya was saying about lacking the resources, we can't just have one person who signs the whole show, because signing like that, they're going to get real tired. You have to identify two or three people for a complete show. I think Pride needs to use more interpreters.

Derek/Onya: Or one interpreter might know a certain song better than another. It's a whole production that's not anything I can control.

Sebastian/Lolita: But back to the question about what things I want to address from my new platform… I want to make this quick and concise. I want to send the same messages that I did at Charlotte Pride, the message of body positivity. If you are giving so much love to me, you can give that same love back to yourself. In a world where there are so many people and so many things out there that are ready to be so hurtful and harmful to you, be that person who wants to be kind to others.

Brooke: That's more than enough. Love it.

Logan/Nova: This kind of relates to the last question, because you brought up HIV prevention and care.

Brooke: And you're at Dudley's Place[2] now?

Logan/Nova: I am. I've been there over a year now. November 28th made a year.

I quickly learned when I started that job that even though we're past the 80s and the 90s and the AIDS epidemic, we're still not that far in the game, and we still have a long way to go. We've been doing a lot of like "lunch and learns" lately about POC communities and how their statistics compare to others, and the

---

2   Dudley's Place is a 501c3 nonprofit organization established in 2019 to serve the support needs of people living with HIV/AIDS.

barriers to care that they experience versus others. So when I was first asked what my platform was as National MX and what issues I wanted to discuss throughout the prelims, my mission statement, if you will, was HIV advocacy. Because in Texas, in New York, I've noticed that there are so many events and shows that offer free testing where you can be tested there on the spot, and in 15 minutes you'll have your results. That's so common. But here it's so taboo to even discuss your status and sexual health because it's been pushed away and so hush-hush for so long that people don't want to openly talk about it. So, that's what I wanted my platform to begin with.

At my prelims, I want to try to partner with local agencies in whatever state I'm in to bring in testing or outreach programs for prevention and PrEP services, and to reduce the barriers to care in whatever local PrEP services already exist. That's one issue that I want to address and not enough people talk about it. We might be 40, 30 years away from the 80s and the 90s, but we are not that far away. I mean, there are no fewer than 25 newly confirmed cases a month here in Charlotte, and actually the number might be larger, it might be 25 per week.

Derek/Onya: And that's only from Dudley's Place.

Logan/Nova: No, that's in general for Mecklenburg County. It's shocking that the numbers are so high and the numbers are largely in our African American female community, the cis heterosexual POC community—women of color who are not English-speaking. These are our new cases and it's sad that we offer all of these opportunities to access care, but haven't eliminated all of the barriers. Something I brought up was that our brochures, like our PrEP brochure, aren't in other languages. That's just one example of something that can be easily overlooked because you're like, Oh, we just need a PrEP brochure. There are just so many things that we overlooked, and that one thing might have helped prevent somebody from contracting the virus.

So that's one of the issues that I want to address. And then another is the general issue of drag being— Drag is mainstream, but also, so many people are actively pushing us back into the closet. And I'm not here for it. We've dealt with it at almost all of our shows for the past year, year and a half, two years, honestly.

And that's where I stand strong. I will not let people do that to us. So now, having a national platform, it's nice being able to talk about the issues that we're experiencing here in North Carolina and in Tennessee and these other states that have tried to pass drag bans, because there are some states and cities where they're just oblivious to what's going on. I mean, you've talked about drag in Texas, and I know that Texas is a difficult state, but a lot of the communities where I've been this year, like Dallas and San Antonio, they had no idea that people in North Carolina were going through protests at every show and death threats. And I'm like, We live it every day.

Derek/Onya: I'm on more hitlists than I ever thought I would be at age 34. Like, being on the Proud Boys' hitlist is insane.

Logan/Nova: It's sad that we have all these brothers and sisters in our community, but traveling has made me realize they don't know what we're going through. But if we make what we're going through known, if we talk about our experiences, then we can have people stand behind us, and there's always power in numbers.

Jaime/Oso: One of the things that you hit the nail on the head about was needing to raise awareness about PrEP in other languages. It wasn't until 2016 that I knew that PrEP even existed. I've been here since '95 and graduated high school. I know the language, and I know a general amount of the law. But I did not know about PrEP. And I'm an English speaker. I know now that there are programs and resources that provide what Dudley's Place and Rosedale provide for free, but a big portion of the POC and the Black and Brown community don't know that all the resources are there. How can we work together collectively to bridge that?

Logan/Nova: It's insane that there are honestly still some agencies that aren't in it for the right reasons. I have a billing collection, currently for $600, from back in Tennessee at ETSU Family Health because I was on a PrEP program and all of their literature—I could probably take a lawsuit against them—but all of their literature says that once you're on this program, all this is covered. They don't discuss time limitations, how long you can be on the program. They say that as long as you're in care and attending all of your booked appointments for a minimum of three months, you're eligible for the program. It wasn't until a year in that I got a bill and it was for the last six months of my care. They were like, "You owe that amount of money because this program was only for six months." Looking back on it now, because I'm at an agency where I'm involved in the grant writing process and see how we get to utilize our money, I understand that ETSU family physicians receive similar funding. They just chose to cut their program off at six months so that they could keep funds for themselves and not invest in the community. It's really disgusting to learn stuff like that. I'm grateful that I had a job where I could look into it, but there are a lot of people who would just say, "Alright, I just have to pay it." So now I'm like, Absolutely not, that's them being selfish. And if that happened to me, I can only imagine how it affects other people who aren't as conscious about stuff like that. It's insane. It makes me proud to work at Dudley's Place and acknowledge the fact that, down to every single penny, the money goes back to our clients.

Jaime/Oso: And even finding queer-friendly doctors—

Logan/Nova: That's what Rosedale prides itself on being, an LGBTQIA+-centered, welcoming health clinic.

Brooke: I have a friend at Triad Health Project, which offers HIV prevention and care, who's been part of transforming the organization this past year. They got a new Cuban Executive Director who brought people of color on board so that the staff look like the communities they're serving. And she's talked about what a huge difference that's made. It's also meant that they were able to obtain more grant money to serve communities.

Logan/Nova: It's crazy that you mentioned that because Rosedale has a very diverse staff. When you approach the reception desk at Rosedale Health and Wellness, you're greeted by a Black woman and an immigrant, Angelica. And most of our nurses are women of color. It's a very diverse crew, even in the lab and the onsite Walgreens. But then when you look at Dudley's Place, we are more white-leaning, which we've been working on. But our mental health therapist is a woman of color. Our new Director of Special Populations is a queer man of color who is also very open about his HIV status. So we do have that welcoming environment where you can see yourself in all of our staff. It wasn't until recently that it was brought to our attention that some of our events looked like they were not very welcoming…

Jaime/Oso: representative of our community

Logan/Nova: representative of our community. But that comes from someone who doesn't really know the organization. When you look at our organization, 80% of our clients are people of color and 45% of our clients are people who do not speak English as their first language. It is a very diverse place. It's just kind of beautiful. People don't see that until you finally put your foot in the door. It's not always in the forefront, but it's also kind of nice because there are other organizations that flaunt it. They're like, Oh, this is all the work we do. It's kind of nice working for an organization that's like, We just do it. We don't have to flaunt it.

COULD YOU DISCUSS HOW TO SUCCESSFULLY CREATE DIVERSE, INCLUSIVE DRAG SHOWS?

Brooke: You've all talked about the importance of diversity and inclusivity in the drag community. Could you talk about how to successfully create inclusive spaces?

Jaime/Oso: I think what a lot of people don't understand is that a lot happens behind the scenes. Just because a show has all white entertainers and all white queens does not mean that the producers or hosts aren't thinking about diversity. All of us here are booked regularly. The fact that we all have this evening off is a rarity.

Sebastian/Lolita: I mean, we did work this morning, so we deserve it.

Jaime/Oso: But a lot of people don't realize that we only know what we know. That's why I'm building a log of Latine performers, new performers, performers of color and making it accessible to the community. Because it may be that we're all booked or the people that you know who you reached out to are booked, so you just go down the list. That's going to happen. But at the end of the day, a lot of people don't realize what happens behind the scenes. I know what happens behind the scenes, so as much as I want POC everywhere, I also have to understand that I cannot in good conscience recommend a Spanish-speaking drag performer in a venue that is not safe. If they are an immigrant, if they don't speak English, if there's no way to protect them, because it's not fair to say to Onya, to Nova, "Hey, I have this amazing artist. Here's their contact information." God forbid something happens at the show because I connected them.

Logan/Nova: Um-hum. And that's how I feel, I know you all know this, about East Frank (Superette & Kitchen in Monroe, NC) because especially when we were going through those protests regularly, all it takes is for the entertainer to not come through the back door because they're new and don't know to do that, or they forgot that I sent them a message, and they come to the front and they're harassed by 20 to 30 protesters.

Jaime/Oso: To the point that we had security.

Sebastian/Lolita: We had to park in the back of the building to make sure that they didn't trash our cars. When we did a show in Albemarle, we had to drive up, take all of our stuff out of our car, and someone would have to drive our cars to another part of town.

Derek/Onya: They drove our cars to the police station, so that they were on police security cameras in case anything happened to them because people were throwing stuff, probably shit.

Outside of Charlotte, Charlotte is such a wonderful city, but you go 30 minutes out of Charlotte and you're in the 1950s. When we were doing shows in Albemarle, and I will say from a place of privilege, I was booking people to make the cast diverse. I wanted the experience to be all the different types of drag you can experience because Albemarle is the equivalent of a food desert, a drag desert, where there's no gay representation that you can see in your hometown. Just being able to go out and drive back home in 10 minutes, instead of the hour and a half that it takes to get from Charlotte to Albemarle. But in that case, I also learned that while yes, these are all the different types of drag I enjoy, it is not responsible of me to put another person— Like we had a Black trans king who literally had a panic attack because of everything that was happening, and to this day, very rarely goes and performs at brunches because of what happened at that show.

Brooke: At a show in Albemarle?

Derek/Onya: Yes. And I do very much take full responsibility for that. That was a lack of judgement. And now I very much have to go through and say, Okay, this is, say, Lake Norman, I have x, y, and z. These are the type of people in a Lake Norman audience. This is what they enjoy. Do x, y, and z performers that I usually use fit? Would any of them be comfortable? There's a whole list of checklists and criteria and then I'll go through and I'll ask them x, y, and z questions. "This is where it's at, this is how much it pays, are you okay with performing in that environment? You have to think about all the different aspects of what could be a danger to someone.

Logan/Nova: Sometimes in providing a welcoming queer environment in a town that doesn't see queer representation, it does come with cons of who is welcome. It's that double-edged sword of we all want fair representation, but if we bring all queer representation, are we going to put certain people in harm's way?

Jaime/Oso: My first time performing in Monroe, I was scared because

Logan/Nova: A.) you were their first king

Jaime/Oso: I was their first king. (laughs) I'm the first king for a lot of shows. I am an introduction to something different than a drag queen. But in spaces like Monroe, Nova had to come and ask me, "Hey, are you okay?" Because, back then, there were, like, five anti-trans bills that they were trying to pass in the North Carolina legislature. One of the bills back in the day was a program here in Mecklenburg County where the police department could ask for immigration papers. If you were stopped at a red light or a checkpoint, they could ask you for them. And if they had probable cause, you would get arrested and detained in an ICE detention center to verify whether you were or weren't a legal resident. Nova came back and she asked, "Hey, is it okay if I touch on the fact that one of the entertainers is unable to vote when I talk about the bills they're trying to pass?", and I was like, "Yeah." Then I walked out there because she'd asked me if I wanted to talk. I talked about my experience. I was scared because I didn't know what the response was going to be. They were welcoming to me as a drag entertainer, but when you're bridging the entertainer and your personal life… There are a lot of walls and barriers that we've put up because we've seen the backlash firsthand. We've read the death threats. We— (Oso looks at Nova) If you want to pick up on this, I'm pretty sure you know what I'm going to say. I don't want to go ahead and put your experiences out there with the stuff that has happened in Monroe, but I was scared because people were finding my friends' government names and addresses and harassing their families. The last thing that I want is for, because I do drag, somebody to find where a family member of mine lives, and something were to happen to them, all because of—

Logan/Nova: It's terrifying. There were a couple of months where protests were so strong that I'm afraid to throw the protesters' names out there. They found my government name. Through my government name, they found my parents' names. They did sleuthing and found out that my father is a pastor. They found out where my parents live and their phone numbers because my mom is not very familiar with social media and unfortunately had her number on Facebook. They went through this whole thing where they started harassing my family because how could they be conservative Christian upstanding members of the community, but allow their drag queen son to sexualize and groom children and molest children and be a pedophile? I felt very responsible for my family being at harm, to the point where it started bringing up triggers from when I first came out, and first came out as a drag queen to my parents and how they felt as if that wouldn't be a good career for me, but then I made advances and won pageants and they were like, Well, maybe this could go somewhere for you. But then all of this happened, where they were being brought into the protest, and taking steps back. It brought up triggers about how that might affect my family dynamic. It was a lot.

I'll admit I bring some of the same entertainers back constantly at East Frank (Superette & Kitchen) in Monroe because they know. We all went through it together. Our core group, we know, you know. We've lived it. And it's our responsibility to look out for vulnerable people, just like Onya said. Why would I put other entertainers in that position even though we are in a better spot now? I assume that responsibility and that's a lot. You know, it's a lot.

Jaime/Oso: It's not just the entertainers we need to protect, but also the people in the audience because when you're creating these safe spaces in these towns and cities that don't have a lot of clear representation— Say a parent brings their trans or non-binary child, and because these towns and cities aren't having these conversations like we are, about our own queerness and safety, all it's going to take unfortunately is for someone to be in the wrong place at the wrong time. And the worst thing that can happen is to, out of the goodness and kindness of your heart, bring a child, or someone who is extremely exploited and marginalized from the queer community, and have a moment or an experience that is life-threatening that would make them make the decision to no longer go to drag shows, to no longer go to open public spaces because they fear for their safety. All it takes is one negative experience.

Logan/Nova: Bringing it back to inclusivity and why that's so important in our community and in the events that we do. Of course, we all put inclusivity at the forefront of our events and the things we produce. However, one of my best friends who is a queen of color from back home in Tennessee really said it best. She said, "Of course inclusivity is going to be at the forefront, but in these minority groups who are sometimes at a higher risk of danger, sometimes the inclusivity is not as important as their safety." Because of course we want them represented, but they have to be here to be represented. That's a harsh truth. But, sadly, in this world that's the truth.

WHAT DOES THIS STATEMENT MEAN TO YOU? "RESIST THE BINARY, ANY BINARY."

Brooke: One of my favorite bookstores, Scuppernong Books in Greensboro, created a shirt that says, "Resist the binary, any binary." What does that statement mean to you?

Sebastian/Lolita: Well, if no one else has any input on this...

Jaime/Oso: Well, as our resident non-binary representative, Lolita Chanel, Mx Charlotte Pride…

Sebastian/Lolita: I speak for all the NB's. Hear my roar, I speak for the Lorax! (Everyone laughs.) I'm not a fan of talking about myself a lot, but to me, Resist the binary, any binary is referring to not letting yourself be defined by what is considered the norm. I say that as someone who asked for years, Where do I stand—am I a man or am I a woman? Am I masculine or am I feminine? In reality, I feel like I'm a combination of both masculine and feminine, but I'm not a man and I'm not a woman. I feel that I live my life as surely as I want to. It's been so freeing coming out as non-binary because I gave up the expectations I had growing up. I grew up thinking that I had to be a man, but now I've freed myself not only from those standards, but also the standards I held myself to as Lolita to be super hyper-feminine. I get to live myself freely and not care that there are moments where I don't appear to be one gender or the other. I am my own experience. And I stand solely on that.

Derek/Onya: To go off Lolita, I think as drag entertainers in general, we're all on the spectrum of fluidity. No one really identifies as one thing or another. Nova's got their nails painted. Oso does whatever he wants and I've always been like—

Jaime/Oso: You always have different hair colors.

Derek/Onya: I always have different hair colors, but also as far as how people address me, I always tell people I go by any pronouns as long as you're not disrespectful. I can tell by tone the moment that you take a wrong turn. And as long as we can be respectful, I don't care what you call me. Just be nice about it. I have no fluidity problems. I'm so comfortable now after being in drag for seven, eight, nine years—I don't even know anymore—that I don't really care how people perceive me. As long as I'm comfortable, I'm happy. Why would it bother you? I don't do "me" for you. I do "me" for me.

Sebastian/Lolita: To be honest, that's been one of the things I loved so much about coming out as non-binary. The main thing that I always hear, and even to this day my own parents say it, "God made man and woman, not—" They haven't said anything like that for a while, but I bring it up because that's the argument we've always heard about people identifying as different genders and using different pronouns. Conservatives make all these really bad jokes about it. There are probably multiple genders out there. If you talk to a scientist in regards to genealogy or chromosomes, there are so many different combinations of chromosomes. There is this woman on TikTok who got very famous because she lived her whole life thinking that she was a man, but eventually came to the realization that she didn't have XY chromosomes. Her specific chromosome combination was, like, XXXXXY. So a lot of her feminine traits, with the combination of having the Y chromosome, led her to have certain different features throughout her life. That was something I thought about myself, like I see people my size or bigger and they have a regular flat chest and I have a voluptuous chest, thank you very much. I had to acquire it somehow. And there are just features about me that, on other men, I don't really see very often. So I think, in a way, I've always been on that spectrum of not so much this, or not so much that, either. And the freedom that comes with it of like, I don't have to explain this to you and you don't have to understand me. You just need to respect me.

Logan/Nova: That's exactly my drag style. People always told me back in Tennessee, and even when I first moved here, they said, "You have to wear a wig, or you have to have the whole illusion of having breasts and the thin waist and the big hips to be booked. That's what drag is, that's what drag queens are." Back in

Tennessee, I kept being told that with my style, I was never going to go anywhere. Well honestly, it's not for them to get. It's for me. I do it for myself. I think it's a true testament of sticking to that, and not conforming to the binary of what people tell me I should do. It's resisting the binary that has put me in the position that I have because I've stayed true to myself. I hold true and prove them wrong. The phrase the underdogs come out on top is true. The underdogs who were told we can't and can't and can't, well, we can. And we will. We'll prove you wrong.

Sebastian/Lolita: I remember seeing a recent statistic that, I think, only 1% of the US population identifies as trans. I mean only 1%, and I have seen so many conservatives making comments and jokes about how transgenders are trying to change society. Look, if 1% was all it took to scare you, then let me tell you about the one percenters, like, let's be honest right now. Where you're being directed to focus is where you're going to make more noise. To be quite honest, if me saying that I'm not a man or a woman bothers you so much at your core, you're protecting yourself. Maybe you're trying to tell yourself something you don't want to acknowledge. I don't know, I'm not a psychiatrist.

Jaime/Oso: I see "resist the binary" kind of like—I'm going to bring in High School Musical, the status quo[1] thing—like yes, we're all in this together. Like, "Resist the system. Any system." That's how I see it. Everything in life is meant to be challenged. Every generation is meant to change, to adapt, to grow. To challenge whatever the existing status quo or binary is, like apart from queerness, the dysfunctional housing system. The dysfunctional education system, the fact that tuition has increased over the last 25 years by what, 200 to 300% in some universities and colleges, but the minimum wage has stayed the same. Rent to income ratios have changed. So it's like all these disparities that are happening, right? The middle class is being dissolved right in front of our eyes. The gap between the poor and the rich is starting to grow and grow and grow. Like, resisting it, but also, I agree with this mentality: work together for a solution. Stop creating that noise. Stop creating that online noise. These keyboard warriors, these social justice warriors that are on top. Because nothing good is going to come of that, and a

---

1   See the *High School Musical* song, "Stick to the Status Quo".

lot of times we're facing life and death situations. Our safety is at risk in our drag shows, in our own homes, and in public spaces. Look at the fact that Tennessee passed a law that criminalized drag[2], essentially making it illegal. The legislation was so loose that if you were in a supermarket wearing a specific type of clothing, you could be criminalized. It's like resist the system, but also understand that as immigrants, as Brown and Black and other marginalized people, we can't do it alone. We need our white counterparts. We need our allies to help. For example, look at the school districts in Cary[3], where every student has a MacBook Pro laptop, versus the D schools[4] here in Charlotte. To me, "resisting the binary" is changing the system, resisting it, but also coming together for a solution. I think that's extremely important.

Brooke: I think it's really interesting that you emphasize coming together for a solution. I recently saw you perform at FUERZAfest[5]. There was a panel discussion between queer Latine artists after your performance, in which there was a lot of talk about the South being at a transition point. Coming from NYC, it feels like people are much more willing to talk across differences to work toward a solution. I would say that attitude contrasts from New York, where everyone is being canceled all the time. Maybe a raging call-out culture is the privilege of moving beyond a certain point, but Niteesh and I have talked about Charlotte being in this transition state where people are still willing to dialogue across differences.

2   On June 3, 2023, a federal judge struck down the Tennessee Adult Entertainment Act, also known as the Tennessee drag ban, a first-of-its-kind Tennessee law that banned drag shows in public or where children could watch them, writing that the unconstitutional measure was passed "for the impermissible purpose of chilling constitutionally-protected speech."

3   According to carync.gov, Cary, NC is a predominantly educated, affluent, and older community that is 57 percent white, 21 percent Asian, 9 percent African American, 6 percent Hispanic, and 7 percent other. It's in the Research Triangle and its public schools generally offer high-quality education, good facilities, and innovative programs.

4   According to the NC Department of Public Instruction, low-performing schools receive a school performance grade of D or F.

5   In 2016, Hispanic Federation launched FUERZAfest, the first LGBTQ+ Latine multidisciplinary arts festival that not only celebrated a vibrant community, but addressed critical issues impacting it.

Logan/Nova: It's funny that you bring up cancel culture. I am both a supporter and hater of it, because I believe in dialogue. I'm a firm believer in calling people out and holding them accountable for their actions and letting them know when they're wrong. But I don't believe that cancel culture should automatically give them no chance of redemption. Like you said, there needs to be a possibility for conversation after a call-out. There need to be conversations to inform them, like, Hey, this is what you can do to change. This is how you can help the community that you may have harmed, or this is how you could, not necessarily redeem yourself, but help right the wrongs that you have done. That's only possible through conversation. People are so quick to just say, Oh, here's where you were wrong. We're done with you because of that, but they're too lazy or unwilling to go beyond that; they just don't care enough to help someone grow. I mean, we're all humans and we all grow together. If we just cancel somebody and leave them there in the dust, like sure they can do the work to try to better themselves, but it's the community and everybody else that can help them along, as long as they want to help themselves. We're all on this planet together. It's all a joint effort of living. You can't just leave someone, if they are willing to learn, if they are willing to help themselves. You've got to be able to extend that olive branch.

Jaime/Oso: What are the changes that are happening here in the South? A couple. I'm going to use an example: I grew up in Tennessee and am currently living in Charlotte. You have a lot of what are considered traditional, Southern-rooted families whose children, now that they're adults, are going off to college and encountering a culture clash between what they were taught at home versus what they're being taught in school. Also, they're moving out of these small towns into more progressive or larger cities that are more receptive to different cultures, people from different backgrounds, and people who speak different languages.

Also, children from marginalized communities are learning to empower each other through social media and the internet. I think one of the funniest examples is when Donald Trump had that one rally and the K-pop community on TikTok said, "Register for a ticket because it's free." The entire stadium ended up being empty, even though in the numbers it had sold out. To think about it, the K-pop community, on TikTok!

Logan/Nova: You brought up children of marginalized communities. I think it's children in general. One of the reasons why these protesters don't want us being in all-age environments around children is because they're scared of what these children are capable of when they get older. My niece is 14 years old, and she is—I'm gonna use this word even though I hate it—woke. She is so woke and involved and aware of the issues that my community faces, and what's going on around her, like the lack of awareness around substance abuse in my hometown, which is something people sweep under the rug, and she's seen that. Children are so smart, and I think that's why protesters don't want us around them. It's not about sexualizing children, it's because we're giving them an environment in which they feel welcome. A place where we're provoking thoughts that expand their understanding of the world. They're going to learn so much about other communities that they might not otherwise be exposed to. Honestly, all of us should be afraid of what children are capable of because we've got this generation of people coming up, who are 10 to 15, who are going to rock our worlds. I wish they were in their 20s; I wish they were able to vote right now. They are going to shake us up.

Brooke: I completely agree. I've worked with students from the Rio Grande Valley on college and scholarship essays for 14 years, and when everything is going wrong in our world, they give me hope.

Logan/Nova: There is hope in the youth of our country. It makes me emotional thinking about it. If my niece has this way of thinking and she's still in small-town Tennessee with my conservative family and her father, who absolutely hates that her uncle is a drag queen and doesn't want her to be involved with me… If she can have these thoughts on her own in that environment, I'm like, Wow. I could never imagine myself at 14 thinking those things because I was still so blinded by everything around me. It gives me hope.

Brooke: You're also saying that social media gives you hope. I think my generation has this doomsday narrative about social media.

Logan/Nova: I cringe sometimes at social media, but at the same time, like Oso said, if the K-pop community could come together on TikTok to give a big "fuck you" to Donald Trump at a rally… The power of social media is both amazing and sad; it's a bittersweet thing. But I think with the power of the youth today and the good ways that social media can be used, like we're not ready. Give us ten years and it's going to be— We just have to stick it out. Some days it's really bleak and we don't have a lot of hope, but then I can read one positive thing and I'm like, Okay, well, it will get better eventually.

Jaime/Oso: Look at the two millennials in the House of Representatives. They are rocking the narrative, the things that they're bringing in. Also, the power of TikTok. Jeff Jackson's been gerrymandered out of his district, but what is he doing? Instead of throwing a hissy fit, instead of going online and bashing his opponents, he's creating TikToks that are educating the residents of North Carolina: What is gerrymandering? And how is it actively happening? Instead of saying, "It is what it is", look for the resources to collectively change things. Jackson knows he's out, there's no changing that. So he's trying to change the system so that it doesn't happen again, or if it does, there are ways to stop it from happening.[6]

Brooke: Speaking of the power of young people and grassroots movements, I think that's part of why I wanted to write about two young people. Country of Under ends in 2007 when Bush was still president. Río is undocumented and queer and DACA wasn't established until 2012. Gay marriage wasn't legalized until 2015. But the beloved community lives in their art and activism, in their trying to make change. I feel that when you all perform. You create these powerful spaces of freedom with your drag shows, where change is very much alive.

6   In the wake of an aggressive Republican gerrymander that all but guaranteed he couldn't have won reelection, Democratic Rep. Jeff Jackson is running for North Carolina attorney general to go after political corruption.

HOW AND WHY DID YOU FORM DKO ENTERTAINMENT? HOW HAS IT ALLOWED YOU TO WIELD COLLECTIVE POWER?

Brooke: Derek, could you talk about how and why you formed DKO Entertainment? (Everyone) How has DKO allowed you to wield collective power (for example, to organize a boycott against The Bar at 316[1])?

Logan/Nova: What does the "O" stand for?

Derek/Onya: Onya

Logan/Nova: Someone asked me and I stood there for, like, the entire day, racking my brain. I thought "Derek Kramer Organization" or "Derek Kramer Opposition"… (everyone laughs)

Derek/Onya: I started drag very non-traditionally. My first few shows in Charlotte were charity-based. I got my first home bar spots doing one show a month at Petra's, doing drag trivia with my drag mom and the person who was my auntie. I didn't really have much guidance, but I also knew that I didn't fit the stereotypical drag queen because I'm not a dancer, I'm not a live singer—

Sebastian/Lolita: Really?

Derek/Onya: Shocking, I know. I'm not a look queen; I am a good time gal. Whereas I don't really fit into the alternative demographic that we think of—like the blood, the gore, the guts, very grungy—being someone who is very comedic and campy is very much alt and a newer thing. Drag has always been camp, but

---

1   Nearly 300 individuals and organizations including Charlotte Pride, Charlotte Black Pride, and Equality NC signed a petition to boycott The Bar at 316 over claims of racism by its bar owner.

you also had to be camp when you could; it was not what you did all the time. Because if you did it all the time, you would never be booked. To get booked, you had to be a pageant queen. Or you had to be a show producer who had the ability to run their own stuff. Until recently, if you weren't doing pageants and winning pageants and actively pursuing pageants, you didn't have a career. This new revolution of drag has really opened doors to be whoever you want to be in the drag narrative, which is a wonderful thing. But it is also kind of limiting. I started in such a non-traditional way that I wanted to collaborate with other artists who weren't very visible because I can honestly say—and this is gonna be a very bold statement, and you correct me if I'm wrong—but until I started producing my own shows, there was no drag king scene that was active in Charlotte. There were male leads, but they weren't anything—

Sebastian/Lolita: respected

Derek/Onya: They weren't anything that you would see regularly. Maybe once in a blue moon, you'd get one that would come up from Columbia (South Carolina) if they fit the right narrative.

Jaime/Oso: I think there were kings; I don't think it was organized.

Derek/Onya: It wasn't organized.

Sebastian/Lolita: You unionized them.

Derek/Onya: Yeah, I unionized them. But there are people like Lolita, who was a dancer but, being plus-sized, also didn't really fit into the other scenes. (To Lolita) But you also were in that weird liminal space where like you were alt, but you were also glamorous, and they didn't know where to put you. You have people like Nova who didn't wear wigs and would wear body suits and capes and pretend to be a superhero half the time. Sorry, Harry Potter half the time. (laughter) But I created a general catch-all of misfits, I guess you could say. The island of lost drag toys.

Jaime/Oso: You created a Glee Club for drag.

Logan/Nova: You were Will Schuester. (Everyone laughs.)

Derek/Onya: Anyways, I treated it more so like bargaining power in the union of Charlotte drag. It allowed us to move into new spaces that weren't typical drag spaces. We do a lot of craft cocktail bars, we used to perform at Common Market on Fridays, so, like I said, drag in unusual places where you don't expect to see drag because honestly, outside of the few places that Vanity House, the other drag house, was, there weren't a lot of other show options outside of 316, Scorpio, and Chasers. It wasn't that I wasn't welcome there, but I also had been doing drag for so long that to go backwards and do a talent show just to get a booking didn't make sense. Where I feel I missed out on a traditional education in drag, I've learned so much more by doing things my own way. A lot of the people who work with us, and I think right now—I just added like five more people—we're at over 100 different entertainers in my Facebook group. I regularly go through that list and post dates each month for availabilities and bookings. That way I have a resource of other misfits.

Jaime/Oso: Can I ask you a question? Because you picked up on something. How do you feel that you have to essentially force yourself into the straight spaces for drag because our own queer spaces are being closed or bought out?

Derek/Onya: I have a love-hate relationship with those spaces, like breweries. Having worked in food service, I know that while the owner may be straight, it's the queer community that helps all of these businesses run, and there's not a brewery that we've done shows in that hasn't had at least one, if not an entire queer staff. I do shows in those spaces because their queer staff should feel represented at work, just as we should feel represented while they are working.

Logan/Nova: It's also an endearing thing to know that we no longer have to rely solely on our queer-exclusive spaces because we are being—I mean, we still have a long ways to go—but we are being more accepted by society. We are being welcomed into more of these spaces. However, it is a sad thing to see our queer safe spaces diminished. It's that bittersweet thing of we have come so far, and we have a long way to go. At least society is welcoming us more, saying, You are valid here. But it does come with that sadness of seeing, because we are integrating more into society, seeing our solely queer spaces not thrive as much. So it's just that bittersweet thing, it's like growing pains.

Sebastian/Lolita: One thing I always praise Onya for is that she has given me the freedom to stand up and call out places like 316 and Scorpio, because I was raised in a generation of drag that believed, Don't bite the hand that feeds you. So it was like, yes, the owner may be racist, but where else are you going to work in the city? Or, you have to be okay with the staff threatening you because where else are you going to find work? Well, along comes Onya, making all of these spaces outside of the gay bars that allowed me to still work and make money without fearing that if I spoke up, I wouldn't work anymore. And I was able to freely stand up and say, These spaces are doing awful things to people in our community and it's time to speak out about it. I have to give my thanks to Onya that I've been able to grow in that way and find the community that I have.

Also, I have so much input in the creative part of shows. I feel comfortable telling Onya, I'm going to be celebrating three years sober, can we do a sober show somewhere? She reached out to coffee shops and found a place that wanted to have a sober show. Charlotte, for the first time in its history, had an all-sober show. I didn't think it would be possible because the only queer spaces we have in the city are gay bars. I couldn't really have a sober show at a gay bar and say, Hey, put away all the alcohol and bring out orange juice for us. That wasn't gonna work. The place where we ended up having it typically sold alcohol, but they didn't sell it during our show; they served coffee all day. We also had an all-Latine cast of people for Hispanic Heritage Month and some of the other holidays on which Latine people should be celebrated. And Onya has not had an issue stepping down at those times to showcase Latine performers.

The people who were running shows in the gay bars were so power hungry—I mean, don't get me wrong, Onya has her moments—(to Onya) love you!—but we have a little control. I will deal with Onya's perfectionism any day over these people who felt like they were God's gift on Earth to drag. Those people believed there was no form of entertainment other than what they were bringing. I will happily take Onya over most of them any day.

Logan/Nova: And dare I say it, we are respected more in these queer-welcoming breweries, craft cocktail bars, and restaurants than we are in our queer-exclusive places. Because for the longest time, the gay bars were so used to seeing drag that it was like, Okay, we're at another Friday night show, and they didn't see the monetary value of investing in our art.

Sebastian/Lolita: In these other venues, you feel the audience's genuine excitement for drag. I can't tell you how many times I've gone out on stage and I'm wearing the same leotard that I wore at a show the night before, but people are jumping up and down, screaming with excitement seeing someone walk on stage like that. Of course, queer spaces should be more welcoming and kinder to their drag entertainers. However, we were not given that kind of respect because old school entertainers and queens wanted to keep the power to themselves, so we went to these spaces that really wanted us there. Like the old saying goes, "Don't go where you're tolerated. Go where you're celebrated."

Logan/Nova: Closed mouths don't get fed.

Jaime/Oso: As a COVID drag baby and the youngest of us four, I'm not sure [my drag persona] Oso would have lasted without these alternative spaces because kings weren't given a spot at Chasers, Scorpio, or 316 (LGBTQ+ bars in Charlotte). But Scorpio would not have lasted as long as it did if it wasn't for the drag entertainers who made that establishment. Same thing for all of these other gay bars, because it was the drag entertainers who brought in their friends and chosen family to support not only the show, but also the bars. The bars, as naturally happens in business once they see an increase in profit, missed a lot of blind spots. They got a little too greedy because they saw an increase in income from bar sales, but they were still paying $25 for two drag numbers. Like, Oh well, we'll continue to exploit drag entertainers. It's like, inadvertently, as a queer community, we were creating our own internal system and we undervalue ourselves so much.

Sebastian/Lolita: A lot of it comes from self-deprecation, but, again, another thing about Onya—I guess… (everyone laughs)

Derek/Onya: I don't like that tone. (everyone laughs)

Sebastian/Lolita: is that she actively makes it her mission to give newer entertainers opportunities to work in venues that otherwise may not have looked twice at them. She is the one who brings in new people, new entertainers, not just new to Charlotte, but new in general. Like Oso said, he would not have lasted at Scorpio or Chasers because they were not kind to kings. Through Onya creating this space outside of the gay bars, they were able to do shows where drag in general is so celebrated. These kings were able to come in and make a name for themselves and do what they needed to do.

Jaime/Oso: It's sad because you would think that in your own queer exclusive spaces, that's the space that you as a queer individual would be celebrated to the max instead of being pushed to the side or exploited or told you know what, your drag will never be—

Logan/Nova: They took it for granted.

Sebastian/Lolita: I was gonna say, you were the prime example of being taken for granted because—

Jaime/Oso: What was the booking fee?

Sebastian/Lolita: Wasn't it like 40 bucks for like four numbers?

Logan/Nova: At my old home bar in Johnson City, Tennessee, the regular pay for their whole cast of entertainers is still $35 to $40 a night and it's four numbers, two shows at 11 (pm) and 1:30 (am). You finish the second show by like 11:45 (pm) and you have an almost two-hour break. It's a very long night. It's a lot of work. It's a big stage. And it's sad. I mean, it just shows— When I told him the manager what my booking fee would be the next time if he booked me, I held firm and he said, "Well, I always tell my entertainers that it's good for them to know their worth." I wanna be like, No, you don't. Because you continuously undermine your entertainers and pay them mere pennies, like $35 is not enough money to buy the foundation that goes on our face. $35 does not cover the fabric that goes into the costume. It does not cover the stones in our jewelry. It does not cover a pair of shoes. I mean, it's just a lot of our queer spaces taking our art for granted and not really acknowledging what they had. You don't know what you have until it's gone. I feel like that's what we're all experiencing: our queer spaces are diminishing and now they're crying for drag and wanting drag.

Jaime/Oso: affordably

Logan/Nova: Correct.

Logan/Nova: And it's like, well, if you would have kept with the times and evolved and valued our art, then you wouldn't be in the situation of make or break. But because of your actions and not growing with us, you know, it's a sad thing, but we're going to continue to find our spaces.

Derek/Onya: Yeah, and we were never meant to be last-ditch efforts or your Hail Mary. We were the foundation.

Logan/Nova: Drag queens and trans women have always been at the forefront of queer rights and queer movements. Let's make that true in our gay bars. We have always been at the forefront of why people come out. They wanted a good night of entertainment, they came out to the gay bar to see a drag show.

Derek/Onya: Where else can you see Liza Minelli with Cher with Dolly Parton mixed with a little Latin boy of drag? Like, why are you crying? Like the things that we used to do, and I do miss it a lot. I found out very early, when going to these new spaces, that my clientele, the demographic that I'm going for, is not gay, it's not drag, because that's just cannibalism. I can't expect queer people and drag entertainers to come out to every show that I produce. I don't even want to go to every show that I produce, but it's my job. But to expect the queer community to come out and support us when we're in non-queer spaces is an unrealistic expectation. That's why some of my biggest fans are cis het women who come out to brunches regularly or come out to the specialty shows that we do in Lake Norman. You have the moms' clubs that are like, This is our weekend activity. We're going to come see drag, we're going to chip in whatever. Hell, I have some church group ladies that come once every three months because they can take a break off of church.

To be an entertainer these days, you have to know so many different facets of the business side of things. Because while yes, it [drag] is a personality, it is a show, if you don't know how to market yourself, you don't know how to talk to people, you don't know how to manage your funds, you aren't gonna go anywhere. That's one of the things that I hopefully have helped teach a lot of the newer ones who have helped me with shows behind the scenes. You have to manage expectations. You have to set realistic goals for venues. You have to say, If you want to do this show and it's not a weekly show, I would like x months for it to become successful because nothing's going to be successful overnight. Or hell, you'll have one really, really good event and then everything else after that will be non-existent. So you pivot, you turn. Drag is such an evolving thing in our community, not just year to year, but day to day. There is always something changing.

THE DRAG IN CHARLOTTE FEELS REALLY MEANINGFUL AND POWERFUL. WHAT DO YOU THINK IS UNIQUE ABOUT PERFORMING DRAG IN THE SOUTH?

Brooke: I moved to Charlotte last year after 20 years in NYC. The drag I've seen in Charlotte feels really meaningful and powerful. What do you think is unique about performing drag in the South?

Logan/Nova: Our lived experiences. We're in the Bible Belt where we were taught to bottle up our feelings because life is easier that way. I think we are a prime example of using art as an outlet for expression and emotion. I know that's why I do it. It's very meaningful because I get to take years of trauma or grief, or just a hard day at work, put my feelings out in front of the crowd, and let them feel that with me. That joint effort of all feeling the same thing for three minutes makes you feel seen.

Jaime/Oso: There's so much cultural history in the South. You have the history of the formation of the United States of America. You have the history of colonization. In Texas, New Mexico, Arizona, there's such a blend of American, Mexican, Chicano culture. That the cultural history here, and the storytelling that has been happening through music— Because artistically, Black artists were not able to perform in white venues. So what did they do? They created songs and art to pass down their stories. I think we are continuing that legacy here in the South. And it's beautiful because it's soulful, it's impactful, and it's everything that I think drag needs, on a nationwide level, to grow and to be more progressive and accepted.

Derek/Onya: You moved to Charlotte in what I would call the renaissance of the South. I've been here 11 years. For a city that's 250 years old, Charlotte's just hit its walking steps. It's being revitalized and the arts have taken off. Over the last six years, public art like murals and other creative expressions have continuously acknowledged historic wrongs toward marginalized communities. Seeing the skyline change and communities find their own spaces has been exciting. When I worked in real estate, I loved hearing why people were moving to Charlotte. Someone would say, "Well, this new company opened, so I'm going to be part of their DEI division." They'd tell me how excited they were to leave their small town because they knew there'd be people like them in Charlotte whom they could impact.

Logan/Nova: Now you rarely meet a Charlotte native. Everybody has a story and they're all from different places.

Derek/Onya: You're more likely to throw a dart in a bar and hit five New Yorkers and one Floridian than someone from Charlotte.

But as far as drag, the Carolinas have been a powerhouse in the pageantry world for years.

Logan/Nova: Look at us now. We have six contestants going to Miss Gay America from North Carolina. We have not seen those numbers in decades.

Sebastian/Lolita: Charlotte, North Carolina, the South in general, we were the pageantry capital of the country. People feared the contestants that came from North Carolina because you really had to work hard to make it in the South. Nobody else had to put as much effort in to go to Nationals. Last year for Nova's birthday, we went to New York, and I was shocked that people there would perform multiple numbers in the same outfits. Whereas I go backstage as soon as my number's done and change my hair, costume, shoes, and jewelry. Sometimes I even change my nails. That's been the standard for us for so long. We were made to put in the work early on in our drag careers. We go to other parts of the country and people are shocked by the fact that we come with different outfits for first number, the second number, tipping, and the final part of the show. The standard here in the southeast is so revered that if we can get past the obstacles, I truly believe that the South will be one of the most powerful parts of this country's drag.

Jaime/Oso: In the drag history of the South, we had a lot of gay men injecting illegal things into their bodies because back then, it was all about the look. It was about the illusion of female impersonation. But if you look at New York City— New York City is such a melting pot of all these different cultures, right? When you take a drag queen from North Carolina up to New York, there's going to be a big culture clash. Vice versa, because in New York, drag truly is art, while here it's more of a protest because of the things that are happening in the South. New York drag is more performative, it's more about entertainment, while here, it's—

Logan/Nova: They do it to entertain an audience. We do it for ourselves.

Jaime/Oso: I'm gonna get that on a shirt. It's survival. We do it for ourselves. New York City—

you go to the West Village, how many queer spaces?

Logan/Nova: Oh my god! One on every corner. I walked through Hell's Kitchen and I was like, Gay bar, gay bar, gay bar, gay bar.

Jaime/Oso: L4 Lounge, which closed recently, was the last lesbian bar in Charlotte. Our queer venues here are fighting to survive, while in New York, they're just competing against each other. Here we're competing against the community.

Logan/Nova: The legislation. The churches.

Sebastian/Lolita: Drive down The Plaza, one of the most progressive streets in Charlotte, and how many churches do we have?

Derek/Onya: But their churches are very progressive.

Sebastian/Lolita: Still, in the South, we have the same number of churches that New York has gay bars. In New York, you want to make a quick dollar? Open a gay bar. In the South, you want to make a quick dollar? Make a church.

Logan/Nova: So Onya, when are you making The Church of Drag?

Derek/Onya: Listen...

Jaime/Oso: Speaking of progressive churches, when Lolita and I went to DC, The National City Christian Church had five banners that made the progressive Pride flag. Seeing that almost made Lolita crash.

Logan/Nova: I would never expect to see something like that. My little Southern Baptist preacher's son heart would absolutely burst and then implode.

Jaime/Oso: The person who booked us said that most of DC's churches are queer-accepting.

Sebastian/Lolita: So maybe the other Christians got it wrong?

Derek/Onya: Well, I mean, obviously.

WHAT'S ONE FUNNY BEHIND-THE-SCENES STORY OR SOMETHING ABOUT YOU THAT WOULD SURPRISE YOUR FANS?

Brooke: What's one funny behind-the-scenes story or something about you that would surprise your fans?

Sebastian/Lolita: Like one particular story that happened, or something we do that's unusual?

Brooke: Either.

Logan/Nova: Something somebody does that's unusual? I'm gonna call Onya out. She doesn't powder her face.

Jaime/Oso: Nova Stella doesn't wear boobs. (Everyone laughs.)

Sebastian/Lolita: I'll one up you. She doesn't wear wigs. (Drag entertainers laugh.)

Logan/Nova: It truly shocks me that Onya sets up an entire number in midsummer and her makeup stays on. Meanwhile, I don't have to do the setup, I arrive in body and padding, and can sweat off my entire forehead. Like, the math doesn't math. It doesn't add up.

Jaime/Oso: One behind the scenes thing happened at Divine Barrel for the Hispanic Heritage Brunch with Hispanic Federation. The first drag queen who I ever saw perform was Angela Lopez. The Hispanic Heritage Brunch was a very full-circle moment because it was the first time that I performed with Angela and we actually got a chance to converse.

I went up to her. I hugged her and I said, "Angela, you were the first drag queen that I ever saw perform. Thank you for inspiring me to do drag as a Latin entertainer."

She said, "Oso, thank you for bringing drag into the future with what you do and for continuing to bring Latin representation."

It took me aback because Angela is a legend—

Derek/Onya: Legend, LEGEND in Charlotte

Jaime/Oso: And to hear those words from the first ever drag queen I ever saw when I was 19, when I walked into that rainbow frickin hallway at The Scorpio onto that big open stage. She was my first drag queen, and to have that moment with her justified, for me as an entertainer, the sacrifices in drag, and also reenergized so much of what Oso is going to do in the future because I still don't know. It's just amazing. I thank Angela so much for that. Because it's very rare that we get to have, I don't know about y'all, but to get to have those full-circle moments, because the majority of the queens that we did see for the first time are no longer with us.

Logan/Nova: Since you didn't go into, like, a funny narrative—

Sebastian/Lolita: This whole time I was like, So what's the joke? (Everyone laughs.)

Logan/Nova: I started thinking about a behind the scenes moment that would shock or empower our fans. A full-circle moment that's a wow factor for me is when I won National MX. Of course, the first people I called were my mom and Hunter. Then I set my phone down. I just wanted to have that moment of like, Holy shit, I did this. When I finally got my stuff together and started telling people bye and thanking them for all of their help throughout the night, I checked my phone. The first text message I saw was a text message from Joey Jay, who is my idol in the Drag Race world. I look up to him because he was very much like the fuck you, like I'm not gonna wear wigs, I'm going to do what I want, but also still give you what you want to see. And it was a wild and very full circle and almost humbling to have the person who I look up to congratulate me on my success.

Then the next day, I had a conversation with my promoter about how Sasha Colby[1] at The Scorpio told me, "Do you know your brand? Do you know how to represent your brand? Then take that to your national pageant and you're gonna be set." I told my promoter about what Sasha had told me and how I carried that through the pageant. He texted her, and she sent a congratulatory message back. I was like, These people who are fucking legends— Sasha Colby just congratulated me. It was so full circle. It's such an empowering thing because if little old Nova Miss Periwinkle from back in Tennessee (everyone laughs) can be congratulated by the icons in our drag community—

Sebastian/Lolita: Sasha Colby truly is like your favorite drag queen's favorite drag queen.

Logan/Nova: Yeah. And the first drag queen I ever laid eyes on and followed on Instagram, Maddelynn Hatter--

Sebastian/Lolita: Ah, same!

Logan/Nova: Her congratulating me, being a friend of mine that I talk to weekly, blows my mind. It's empowering. If little Nova the underdog Miss Periwinkle from back in Tennessee can be congratulated by these entertainers on successes, then like what can you all do? The opportunities and possibilities are endless.

[Onya's funny story has been struck from the record. You'll just have to ask her.]

Logan/Nova: If I had to think of a funny moment, it wasn't me, but it happened at my first weekend booking with Jacqueline St. James, Ida Carolina, and I think it was Sabrina Nox. Jacqueline St. James goes out there and does one of her bucket numbers. She's a big girl, she out there dancin' and—

Sebastian/Lolita: shakin' them titties from left to right.

Logan/Nova: Well, speaking of titties, we're all out there watching her and she has no clue about anything costume-wise going on. She did one of her twirls

---

1   Sasha Kekauoha/Sasha Colby was crowned the winner of season 15 of RuPaul's Drag Race in 2023. Charlotte's LGBTQ+ nightclub The Scorpio hosted Sasha Colby on Friday nights before it closed in October 2023.

where she follows her hands over and spins in a circle, and then pops out of it real quick. Well, when she popped out, her right tit popped out, too. She walked around the entire place and never looked down, never acknowledged it. People are just like living, but she thinks they're living cuz she's dancing. She comes backstage and she walks up those stairs and we're all standing there in the doorway, like, Oh my god, Jackie, pull it up. She turns to the mirror and just pulls the other one out. We were like, Ma'am, you just went out there and gave them a whole show. And she has like massive top-top. Like be careful because if they hit you, you're knocked out.

Sebastian/Lolita: That reminds me of one of the funniest things that ever happened with our good friend Teri Lovo, whose help has made things possible for all of us in this room. When I first started, I was booked at L4 before it became my show. Teri Lovo was booked with me. I remember I finished my number, and I'm going backstage and I hear yelling and I'm like, What is going on? And when I go backstage, Teri Lovo is head-to-toe naked, ready to fist-fight someone because she wanted another drink.

Jaime/Oso: That sounds like Teri. (laughs)

Sebastian/Lolita: She had the most Popeye stance, with her fist up like this, and I'm like, You don't have on clothes, lady. This is a 100% genuinely sweet person, nicest person you'll ever meet, she can barely hurt a fly. To see her in that state, just mind you, biggest cheeks, large titties and just hanging it all out there. Just really fully ready to swing on someone and I'm like, Teri, you literally just took off your gown, you had nothing under your gown? She was just out there, just like living. I'm like, Well, welcome to drag.

FREEDOM
TUNNEL
PRESS